We are
what we thin
All that we are
arises with
our thoughts.
With our thoughts
we make the world.
~ BUDDHA
MW01622988

A YEAR OF GUIDED MEDITATIONS:
52 WEEKLY AFFIRMATIONS

Creative Director: Dudley Evenson
Cover and Design by Bob Paltrow Design
Photography by Dudley Evenson
Photos of Dudley & Dean Evenson by Brett Steelhammer

Printed in the UNITED STATES OF AMERICA
ISBN-10: 0-9991379-2-1
ISBN-13: 978-0-9991379-2-5

Library of Congress Control Number: 2020947510

Published by:
Soundings of the Planet
PO Box 4472, Bellingham, WA 98227
www.soundings.com

For press inquiries, email:
music@soundings.com

NOTE TO READER: This book is intended as an informational guide. The approaches, tools, and techniques described here are meant to supplement, and not to be a substitute for, professional medical care or treatment. They should not be used to treat a serious ailment without prior consultation with a qualified health care professional.

Dudley Evenson

A Year of Guided Meditations

52 Weekly Affirmations

PRELUDE

Welcome to your best year ever. We are excited to offer you this collection of weekly affirmations based on the values and principles that Dean Evenson and I have lived by for over half a century! We see them as universal laws of nature, and we feel that living by these principles has contributed to our meaningful life – both in terms of our long and loving relationship and in regard to running our successful business.

These profoundly positive principles are based on practical wisdom and the book is designed so you can begin your year anytime and focus on a new meditation each week. You can think of them as *Be-Attitudes,* ideals to strive for, inspiring you to become your highest self. We don't claim to have mastered them all, but we do know that contemplating them is beneficial so the principles ultimately become an integral part of who we are.

We hope they help bring the many aspects of your being into balance and harmony. With repetition and intention, these statements can become incorporated in your daily existence and ultimately help focus your mind toward your highest ideals and vision for your life. May these gentle yet powerful reminders help move your thoughts to a higher state so you can live your best possible life.

Here are several ways to use the affirmations to enhance your inner life:

- Start at the beginning of the book and focus on one affirmation at a time, repeating it every day for the entire week as you contemplate that principle or ideal.
- Read the book in its entirety and let each of the affirmations sink deeply into your subconscious mind.
- Do a daily reading by opening the book randomly and focus on the meditation you turn to.
- You can also memorize the short affirmation at the top of each page, and say it to yourself throughout the day.

With perseverance, repetition, and your steadfast belief in them, the words of the affirmations become a part of you. Before long, you look around and realize you are actually achieving what you may have thought was impossible only weeks or months before. Whatever way you choose to use them, we hope these affirmations will benefit your life beyond measure.

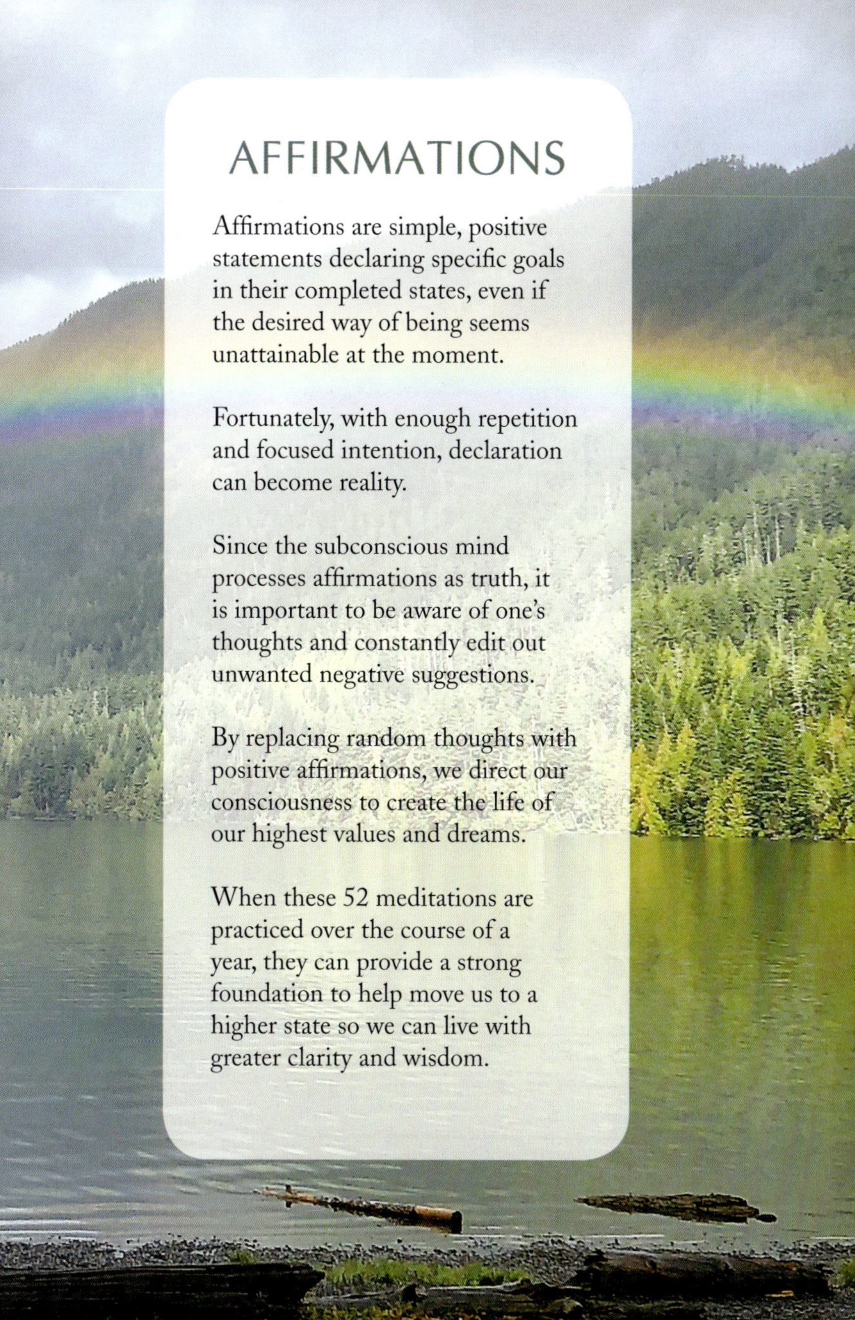

AFFIRMATIONS

Affirmations are simple, positive statements declaring specific goals in their completed states, even if the desired way of being seems unattainable at the moment.

Fortunately, with enough repetition and focused intention, declaration can become reality.

Since the subconscious mind processes affirmations as truth, it is important to be aware of one's thoughts and constantly edit out unwanted negative suggestions.

By replacing random thoughts with positive affirmations, we direct our consciousness to create the life of our highest values and dreams.

When these 52 meditations are practiced over the course of a year, they can provide a strong foundation to help move us to a higher state so we can live with greater clarity and wisdom.

CONTENTS

1 A NEW DAY

I let go of the old and open myself to the new

I sit quietly and center myself,
breathing deeply and fully.

I feel myself firmly connected to the Earth
as I let the spirit flow through me.

I let go of busyness and of anything
that may be overwhelming me.

I open myself to the new,
to new possibilities, to a new day,
and to the fresh new cells being
constantly created in my body
with every breath I take.

I feel the refreshing inspiration
of new opportunities coming my way.

I welcome this new and
wonderful time in my life
and see it filled with goodness,
creativity and peace.

I let go of the old and allow the new
to come gently into my life.

Often, we tend to cling to old patterns and habits that may be holding us back. It is these attachments that can keep us from living fully. In this centering affirmation, we allow ourselves to open up to the many blessings that exist within the vast sea of infinite possibilities surrounding us.

When so-called negative experiences present themselves, we frequently tighten up and form an armor of resistance around us, thereby closing ourselves off from the magic inherent in the unknown.

By always being open to new possibilities, we allow the Universe to harness all its forces to help us in the best ways possible.

This affirmation is a wonderful way to begin our year of weekly wisdom meditations.

2 BREATH

I revitalize myself with every breath I take

I sit up straight with my spine erect but relaxed.

I take a deep breath, inhaling fully, holding for a moment and then exhaling slowly and completely.

I feel the energy my breath brings to
every cell and molecule of my being.

Inhale. Hold. Exhale.

Exchanging energy.

Bringing in fresh, new, life giving energy.

Letting go of what is old and used.

My breath is bringing in the life force.

I let go of what is unneeded. In and out.

With each breath, I am restoring
and revitalizing myself.

I am completely refreshed
with each breath I take.

I am healthy. I am alive.

Without breath, there is no life. Breath carries the life force. Even the plants breathe and thankfully for us since they exhale the oxygen that we inhale to live. Most people use only a third of their lung capacity which means many are living at only 30% capacity. When we are uptight, anxious or worried, we often breathe even less or may find ourselves actually holding our breath. That is why we include this breathing affirmation near the beginning of our process since breathing deeply and fully is the foundation of a healthy body and spirit. Pranayama, kundalini yoga and even the Lamaze method of natural childbirth all focus on the breath for self-empowerment and overcoming pain. Now is the time to incorporate good breathing practice into our daily life.

I am relaxed even during times of stress

I inhale deeply as I tighten all the muscles
in my face, squeezing my eyes, mouth and cheeks.
Hold for a moment and then exhale
as I relax those muscles completely.

Now I breathe in and tighten the muscles
in my neck, shoulders, and chest.
Hold for a moment. Then exhale and release.

Now I breathe in and I make fists with both hands
and tighten all the muscles in my hands and arms.
Hold those muscles tightly and then exhale and relax.

I now focus on my abdomen, hips and buttocks
as I breathe in and tighten all those muscles.
Hold that tension and then release and exhale.

I breathe in and focus on my legs and feet
tightening all the muscles in that part of my body.
Tighten and then release and let go as I exhale.

Now I inhale and tighten all the muscles in my
whole body, every part from face to feet.
Hold that tension and then release as
I exhale and relax completely.

I let my breathing return to normal
and stay in this relaxed state as long as I want.

Research has shown that being relaxed can help one heal. Disease means 'lack of ease' so with that in mind, returning to our natural state of balance should be a goal of a healthy lifestyle. In this exercise of alternating tension and relaxation, we learn what it feels like to be relaxed by experiencing its contrasting state of tension. When people are uptight and tense, they often create blockages within the body system which may cause toxins to accumulate and disease can result. The body and mind are interconnected so when one experiences tension in the mind, it is reflected as constriction in the body. By being aware of the need to relax and by practicing these relaxation techniques, one can mitigate the effects of chronic or acute stress and even pain.

4 PERFECTION

I honor the perfection of the universe

I live in a perfect universe.
Everything in my life works perfectly.

I am in harmony with my world.

I peacefully accept what happens to me
and release what I don't need.

I focus on creating the kind of life I want
and draw that energy toward me.

I take actions that move me in the direction I want to go.

Life is good and I am fulfilled in so many ways.

I experience radiant health and peace of mind.

I have quality relationships and meaningful activities.

I am growing and evolving in ways that excite and fulfill me.

With every step I take, I experience
support and encouragement.

I appreciate the gift of my life.

We often try to control the Universe by wishing things were different than they are, but when we look deeply into the nature of existence, we find the perfection inherent in everything that happens. We tend to judge and quantify events, people and situations, but by so doing, we block the opportunities that may be destined to come our way. This process of accepting the idea of perfection can be difficult at times, especially when sickness, loss, accidents or even death are part of the equation. By truly believing in the ultimate perfection of all that is, we embark on a journey that moves us in the direction we want to go. We may not see the perfection just yet, but by focusing on it, surely we evolve into the divine vision for our lives.

5 HEALING

I radiate health and well-being

I focus on radiant health in body, mind and spirit.

I accept the condition of my health with love
no matter what my mind or
the external world tells me about it.

I make choices that enhance my health and well-being.

I choose foods that support me and I love eating
natural, whole foods that are good for me.

I enjoy a daily exercise routine that stimulates and uplifts me.

I focus on maintaining healthy, supportive thoughts.

I breathe in health. I exhale any residue of negativity.

I radiate a sense of vitality and strength.

I am a perfect picture of health.

As I focus on my perfect health,
any issues or concerns I have gradually melt away.

I am completely and fully alive.

The messages our mind sends to our body have a great impact on the condition of our health. That is why this affirmation is so important, especially if we feel sick or have been 'diagnosed' with an illness or disease. Not only do we need to take actions and make choices that support our health on the physical plane, but we need to be vigilant about what we tell ourselves about the state of our health. Seeing ourselves as radiating health is paramount to actualizing a state of health. Appreciating and focusing on the gift of life will carry us a lot further than complaining about our aches and pains or worrying about a medical diagnosis. Gradually we become what we focus on and in this case, may it be a perfect state of health.

6 ATTRACTION

I attract what I need into my life

I am a magnet for all that is good in the world.

I attract what I want
and I'm filled with life's blessings.

I focus on love and
attract love into my life.

I focus on joy and a sense of joy fills me with its presence.

I focus on peace and my world is full of peace,
both inside and out.

I focus on prosperity
and I have what I need and more.

It is easy for me to share my gifts.

The more I give the more I receive of life's infinite blessings.

My relationships continue to improve and
I attract wonderful friends into my life.

I focus on creating a perfect life for myself and
for those around me and that is exactly what happens.

The Law of Attraction is often misunderstood as a technique for getting rich or attracting a partner. Those might be side effects of positive projection, but the fact remains, this principle is constantly at work in our lives. If we notice that some aspects of our lives are not what we think we asked for, we should look again and listen to our inner thoughts. Then we will understand that all of our reality is linked to our self-generated thoughts and feelings. Being ever aware of what we are projecting, we can change our mind to meet our true vision of life. Knowing that we do magnetize people and events to us, we will become clear on what it is we truly desire and attract what is good and wonderful to us.

7 RELEASING

I let go of what no longer serves me

I release and let go of that which no longer serves me.

I let go of unnecessary thoughts and things.

I let go of grief and sadness.

I let go of judgment of others and especially of myself.

I let go of expectations of how I think it should be.

I let go of needing to be right.

I release feelings of lack and fear.

I have enough of what I need.

I let go of relationships that no longer serve me.

I am supported in all ways.

I easily and freely release and let go of thoughts, feelings, and attachments that are not helpful to my being the very best person I can be.

I let go of anything that is holding me back from fulfilling my life's purpose. I am free.

Letting go can be very difficult but it is absolutely essential to moving on. There are many aspects of letting go that we need to address. It may be a relationship or it may be an expectation or it may be the loss of a thing, of something we treasured. It is interesting to note that sometimes when we are truly able to let something go, it may actually return to us. That does not mean we should expect that to happen, but it might help the process. The main thing to understand about releasing is that without truly letting go, we are blocking opportunities and relationships coming to us that could be beneficial to us. Honest releasing makes space for something even better to come into our lives

8 CREATIVITY

I welcome the creative spirit to flow through me

I open myself to the creative flow of
the universe to channel directly through me.

I allow my eyes, ears, mouth and hands
to be tools of the universe to create through me.

I joyfully create a beautiful life for
myself and for those around me.

I apply my innate creativity to everything I do.

I specifically welcome the creative spirit
to touch the areas I am passionate about.

I welcome the discipline that it takes
to achieve success in my chosen areas of creativity.

I am inspired by those around me and in turn,
I become an inspiration to people whether I know them or not.

I joyfully create and send forth my creations into the universe.

Everyone is creative whether they are an artist, a parent, a homemaker, a business person, a teacher, a maid or truck driver. Each person brings something of the creative spirit into the various aspects of their lives. It is important to honor and appreciate the gifts and talents we do have and work to enhance and develop them. Many people tend to discount their innate creativity by saying they aren't creative, can't sing or draw a straight line. Well, I have news for you. Art doesn't always happen in straight lines or perfect pitch. It occurs when the spirit is freed to be itself by allowing joy and passion to be expressed. Creativity happens in many ways.

9 PURPOSE

I act in harmony with my purpose

I know that my life
has meaning and purpose.

I am coming to understand why I was born.

I am discovering my gifts and talents and in the process,

I am able to have a clearer picture of how
I can use my gifts to bring greater meaning to my life.

My passion for life is increasing as I discover
how I can best be used as a force for good in the world.

As I continue to apply myself
in the areas of my passion,
I find greater clarity of the big picture
of who I am and what I have to offer.

I peacefully accept myself and trust
that my life is unfolding according to plan.

I am a co-creator of that plan.

Why were we born? What is the purpose of our lives? Some say it is to experience love and joy. For sure, we know that each person is born with a unique set of gifts and talents. Discovering those gifts may be a life long journey, a process of unfolding as we seek to understand who we are in our unique magnificence. If we have been avoiding this question and have wandered into areas that conflict with our inner essence, perhaps now is the time to return to these ultimate questions. Sometimes just asking the questions will allow the answers to be revealed. In any event, it is always good to stimulate a passion for life and enhance the process of understanding one's personal purpose and mission.

10 GRATITUDE

I am grateful for all without conditions

I am grateful for the gift of life
and all my many blessings.

I am grateful for family and friends and
a place to live and food to eat.

I am grateful for the earth
and the spirit of life.

I am grateful for the sun that shines every day
and for all the life it creates.

I am thankful that I can learn and grow from experiences
I may not even have wanted, but that allow me to
open up to a greater awareness of myself and my world.

I am grateful for love
that flows to me and through me.

I see all as support
for the journey that is my life.

So often we wait to have what we want before feeling thankful. In this case, we may be waiting a long time. To jump-start the flow of blessings in our life, we practice gratitude at all times, even for the things that might appear negative. When we can be truly grateful for everything that happens, the good or the bad, we will find that our lives gradually improve. It may be challenging at first to find the silver lining in every situation, but once this habit of gratitude becomes a part of us, we will be pleasantly surprised by what opens up for us. We can begin by expressing appreciation for the basics like food and shelter and for small things that we can easily acknowledge. From there, we can allow our gratitude to grow and when it does, we shall be ready for even better things to come our way.

11 LOVE

I give and receive unconditional love

I am open to love flowing to me and through me.

I open my heart to all, without conditions.

I give and receive unconditional love.

I send out love to my family,
to my community, to my world.

I offer my love to those who might be
considered my enemies and they become my friends.

I send out love to myself –
to my body, mind and spirit.

I accept myself unconditionally
in all my magnificence.

I breathe in love, I breathe out love.

Love fills me with its joy and support.

I am nurtured in unconditional love.

I let go of loneliness and let myself be
bathed in the fulfillment of precious agape love.

Giving and receiving unconditional love needs to become as basic to us as breathing in and out. The heart is the center of our circulation system where energy is transformed and carbon dioxide and oxygen are exchanged. Nothing happens without the other so if we wish to be loved, the best action we can take is to give love. By turning our focus toward giving love to others, we open ourselves to be the recipients of love. One of the greatest challenges we face is being able to truly love those we may not even like or those whom we consider to be enemies. The honest expression of love can transform animosity into friendship, hatred into love, and threat into support. In the process, we need to also remember to love ourselves.

12 RELATIONSHIPS

All my relationships are harmonious

I am in harmony with my world.

I am in harmony with those around me,
with my family, my community, my world.

I create balance in all my relationships.

I feel my connection to the earth,
to the human family, to the spirit.

I relate well to
those who are close to me.

I take responsibility for my part in healing family histories
that may have carried over many generations.

I notice my patterns and work on myself lovingly
to overcome anything that might hold me back
from having completely harmonious relationships.

I accept myself and others with love and compassion and
the quality of my relationships is constantly improving.

Everything in our world is built around relationships. We relate to ourselves, our parents, partners, family, work associates, community members, earth and spirit. How we negotiate the complex web of interconnection determines how well we function in the world and how we feel about ourselves. The foundation of a successful life depends on the success and harmony of our relationships The more we can take responsibility for our own part in the quality of our relationships, the more likely we will be able to correct or clarify anything that might be a blockage to getting along with others. As our relationships improve, we will notice all the aspects of our lives improving.

13 FAMILY

I feel unconditional love for my family

I honor and respect my family of birth
or the family that I grew up with.

I accept my position in my family.

I honor my parents for who they are and
accept without conditions how I was raised.

I acknowledge any judgments I might still have
and gently let them go.

I move forward in my process and forgive the past.

I forgive my parents and their parents for their shortcomings.

I forgive myself for my own shortcomings.

I send out unconditional love to all my relatives.

I let my love extend beyond my blood family and
feel my connection with my tribal roots
and with the whole human family.

I accept who we are and focus on
who we can become in our highest manifestation.

The issue of family can be difficult for many. Family karma often carries on from one generation to the next and will show up in surprising ways, reminding us to pay attention to the habits and ways of being we may have inherited. With vigilant awareness, we can actually heal our personal and familial karmic patterns. We can also heal our relationships with our parents, even if they have already passed on. And of course, healing our relationships with our living family, our siblings and our children can be the bonus of a lovingly aware life. Beyond our blood family exists our tribal family and our families of choice. Letting go of judgments and any sense of separation can help in feeling connected with the whole human family.

14 COMMUNITY

I feel part of an extended community

I feel connected to my community.

Whether it is my family, work group, small village or large city, I relate to this group of people in meaningful ways.

I realize our interdependence and honor the many ways we contribute to one another's well being.

I am constantly looking for ways
I can be of service to those around me.

I notice those in need
and offer my support.

I accept help from others
when I find myself in need.

I enjoy participating in community events
whether they are social, spiritual or work related.

I strive to be a contributing member of my community and enjoy the sense of teamwork and purpose that can be achieved when working together as a group.

No man is an island, no man (or woman) stands alone. We are each a part of a greater community that exists beyond our personal family or tribe. As we rebuild the fabric of our communities, we will see how we all fit together, each contributing to the health and well being of the whole. As we discover our gifts and talents and acknowledge our own skills and resources, we will be able to help those in need and at the same time, be able to benefit by their services and resources when we are in need. By reaching out beyond our immediate world, we will receive great benefit and fulfillment and probably have a good time too.

15 INNER PEACE

I access inner peace in any situation

I allow myself to go to a place
deep inside where peace resides.

I lovingly let go of disturbing thoughts
and feelings that are holding me back.

I forgive people and events that may
have caused me pain in the past.

As I forgive and let go, I notice a sense of
comfort surrounding me and replacing any
negativity with positive feelings.

I sink deeper into this experience of peace and security.

I feel a sense of trust and acceptance growing within me.

I am learning to connect with my inner core of peace
even when events and people around me feel overwhelming.

I feel joy in the realization that inner peace is always
available to me, no matter what is happening in the world.

It is exciting to realize this basic principle – that no matter what is happening in the outer world, one can access a deep core of peace within. Often, we are waiting for things to settle down in our world before we allow ourselves the blessing of inner peace. This is a backwards way of dealing with life. The fact is, we want to begin with inner peace and from that place we will extend out and spread peace into our immediate world and plant seeds of peace that can extend to a world beyond our imagination. Being in a state of peace does take practice, so focusing on this affirmation regularly when we are in a fairly calm state will train us to access it when things get stirred up around us.

16 WORLD PEACE

I see the world becoming more peaceful every day

I recognize the world for all its drama as a
reflection of my own inner experience.

As I work to change my perception of the world,
I realize I am actually affecting the world around me.

As I change how I am seeing the world,
the world changes with me.

I see beauty around me.

I see the goodness in people
and honor them for that goodness.

I even practice seeing our own
national/political world in a different light.

I see it as a process and I focus on the evolution of
human consciousness as we move toward greater
awareness and compassion.

I see the world becoming more peaceful and just every day
as I myself become more peaceful and fair within.

When one pays too much attention to mainstream media, it is easy to feel overwhelmed by the constant barrage of negative news.

It is therefore important to turn one's focus toward more uplifting and inspiring information about the state of the world. There is always something good and wonderful to focus on but it does take self-discipline to stay positive.

By looking at the state of the world in a historical context, it is often possible to see how far humans have come and how much has been achieved in terms of our values and principles.

When we become more peaceful within, we have a more beneficial influence on those around us and our own world becomes more peaceful.

17 TRUST

I trust that everything works out for the best

I trust that my life is evolving perfectly.

I accept the world as it is
while still striving to
improve it however I can.

Even though I may have experienced
injustice or harm in the past, I am
cultivating within me a sense of trust
that things eventually work out for the best.

With a faith in the healing power of time,
I move forward in my life without blocking the
goodness that is destined to come my way.

I let go of fear and blockages
and open to acceptance.

I trust in a positive outcome
to all circumstances and events.

I have faith in the universe to provide the lessons
and support I need to be my very best.

There is a fine balance between trusting that everything will work out and taking actions to help make it happen. It is important to come from a place of trust while at the same time, taking meaningful steps to move things along. By having a trusting spirit, we affirm our partnership with the universe and place ourselves in a better position to improve our lives and overcome temporary hardships or disappointments. With time and faith, there is no loss or negativity that can't be overcome. This does not mean that we can know the exact nature of how our lives will unfold or that everything we wish for will happen, but it does allow us to accept things as they come and learn the lessons that are being offered to us.

18 FORGIVENESS

I welcome forgiveness to wash over me

I forgive those I feel may have harmed me,
either knowingly or unknowingly.

I forgive my parents and those closest to me
who may have treated me in ways I didn't like.

I forgive whole groups of people who
I may believe have acted wrongly.

I especially forgive myself for anything I may ever have
done that doesn't measure up to my values and beliefs.

I forgive events beyond my control
that may have caused me grief or loss.

I lovingly let go of judgments that are holding
me back from enjoying life at its fullest.

As I learn to forgive, I open myself to a
glorious feeling of release and acceptance.

I find the greatest result when I lovingly
forgive and accept myself as I am.

Forgiveness is difficult but essential to letting go of the grip negative experiences have on the psyche. When a person is angry with someone who has inflicted pain or harm, they often think they are holding that person accountable. On the contrary, what they are really doing is hurting themselves. Often the perpetrator of the harm is oblivious to the situation, and the person holding the anger is the one letting negativity eat away at their soul and creating a climate for sickness and disease to take over. Forgiveness is necessary to move forward in one's life and free oneself from the bondage to the situation that needs to be released. True forgiveness will allow the pain of the past to finally disappear.

19 SERVICE

I find creative ways to be of service

I strive to be of service to my family,
my co-workers and my world.

I enjoy being helpful and
giving of myself to support others.

I look for ways I can offer my skills and
talents to make the world a better place.

I am creative in finding
ways to give of myself.

I am not looking for appreciation when I offer
my services, but rather I am simply making myself
available to assist those in need.

As I give of myself, I find that I receive a great deal
in return, not in terms of recognition, but simply in my
enjoyment of being able to help.

Being in service is contagious and the more I serve,
the more others find ways of serving as well.

If we can all learn to serve each other, we will discover that everyone has what they need. Being of service to others is one of the most profound gifts we can give for when we serve others without need of recognition, we are truly giving of ourselves. There are so many people in our world in need of both physical and spiritual support that once we begin to look for ways we can contribute to others, the answers will be right in front of us. We can serve in ways both large and small, depending on our capacity and abilities. The benefits to others are obvious. The benefits to ourselves may be subtle, but great blessings come when we give of ourselves in meaningful ways.

20 FULFILLMENT

I am fulfilled in all ways

I feel the spirit of life
filling me with its blessings.

I am fulfilled in all aspects of my life.

I feel satisfaction in the quality of my relationships.

I am fulfilled in my daily work, whether it is
the ultimate work I shall do or not.

I am creatively and spiritually fulfilled
in the many areas of my life.

I even find appreciation in the details from
washing the dishes to doing other necessary chores.

I search for opportunities to explore new territories
and discover new aspects
so I may extend myself in greater ways.

I feel the richness of life all around me as
I open myself and expand my horizons.

When we focus on what is lacking in our lives, we are unlikely to experience a sense of fulfillment. Therefore, it makes sense for us to turn our attention away from lack and toward awareness of the abundance and gifts of life. When we come from a place of appreciation of our blessings, even in trying times or in the midst of hardship or trauma, we will find that we are better able to attract to us the blessings that we crave. This is one of those affirmations that we need to remind ourselves of frequently and use especially in times that don't seem to be exactly what we would have wished for. It is also good to use this affirmation during tedious activities as it will even help us get through boredom or frustration.

21 JOY

The spirit of joy fills me up

I let my heart sing with joy.
I welcome joy into my life.

It is easier than I realized
to experience joy's healing power.

Joy fills me up,
revitalizing every cell and molecule of my being.

I breathe in joy
and breathe out sorrow and suffering.

I am happier than I have ever been before and
don't even need a reason to feel this way.

I laugh a lot and enjoy even the mundane aspects of my life now
that joy has become a part of me.

My newfound joyful nature attracts people to me
who are also joyful and our mutual happiness increases.

Life is wonderful.

Often, we spend our whole life waiting for something magnificent to happen before we allow ourselves to feel joy. Then we wonder why we keep waiting for so long to feel happy. When one consistently comes from a joyful place, all sorts of good things happen and we attract wonderful people and events to us. Notice how children live in a state of joy and don't need anything in particular to make them happy. Of course, it is helpful if basic needs are fulfilled, but beyond the basics, we can operate from a place of joy at all times, not just when we think everything is worked out and in its place. By maintaining our joy, we will be pleasantly surprised to find we can maintain a level of happiness all the time.

22 FRIENDSHIP

I am grateful for the blessing of friends

I honor and respect the friends I have.

I appreciate the support that good friendship brings.

I reach out to others in friendship and
in turn, receive their blessings.

If I find myself alone or feeling lonely,
I don't think about my own situation,
but instead try to reach out to
someone else who needs support.

In the process of becoming a better friend to others,
I find that people treat me in a more friendly way.

I extend myself in friendship to all sorts of people,
young and old, near and far, familiar and unfamiliar.

I am surrounded by loving people in a very friendly world.

I feel safe and supported.

Whether we have one friend or many, we treasure that connection with other humans. We also appreciate and enjoy the friendship of animals. As we learn to be a good friend and reach out to others in a giving spirit, we will find that the depth of our associations increases and we will attract more quality relationships into our lives. Instead of dwelling on loneliness or lack, we can decide to reach out and share the gift of who we are with others who may need a friend. As we learn to give more of ourselves, we will find that people notice and appreciate us and are more likely invite us into their lives. Let us also remember how we like to be treated and treat our friends in loving and thoughtful ways as well.

23 SPIRIT

I am filled with the spirit of life

The spirit of life fills me up.

My cup overflows with the bounty of life's many blessings.

I take in a deep breath and know that
I am breathing in the life force.

I exhale and my out breath nourishes the plant kingdom.

I am aware of a sense of balance that pervades the universe.

I appreciate that I am a part of that balance.

I am a channel for the spirit to flow through.

I am the individualized hands, feet, eyes, ears,
mouth and mind of the great spirit of life.

I take care to act and think responsibly as
I carry this precious spirit within me.

It is a great honor and privilege to be alive
and I act in a way befitting this honor.

With every breath we take, we invite the life force into our being. We recognize the interconnected relationship between us and the world around us. The living spirit pervades everything. As the individualized expression of this spirit and through our uniqueness, we carry a great responsibility to live in a way that reflects the majesty of the life force. What we do, say, and think carries a power beyond our imagination so with this in mind, we need to consider thoughtfully how we act in all ways. Everything we do has an effect so as carriers of this life force, we make choices that will achieve the greatest benefit for all concerned. Whenever we feel weak or small, we need only remember to breathe.

24 INTENTION

I am in tune with the intention of my life

I am one with the intention of my life.

I am attuned to the higher intention of the universe and I flow easily along with it.

As a result, doorways open up for me and things fall into place.

My life functions smoothly and successfully.

As I open to my life's purpose,
I focus my intention on
the direction I want to go.

I achieve my goals easily.
I am able to make decisions and take actions
that achieve the results I want.

I find meaning in even the smallest things and
I am imbued with a greater sense of purpose for my life.

When we can harmonize our personal intention with the intention of the universe, we will find that things fall into place and we can easily achieve our goals and manifest our dreams. This doesn't necessarily mean we narrowly focus on one thing or another. Instead, our lives will function more smoothly when we broaden our intention to include the many exquisite facets of our being in a whole and complete way. As we learn to fine-tune our intention, we will discover that life can unfold more easily and with a greater sense of order and divine perfection. We will be pleasantly surprised to discover aspects about ourselves that we didn't realize were there and in so doing, we will grow in new and exciting ways.

25 FOCUS

I focus on what is good in my world

I realize that what I focus on expands.

I therefore choose to focus on what is
good and beautiful in my world.

I focus with gratitude on what I have in life
rather than on what might be lacking.

In the process of acceptance,
many blessings come my way.

If I notice a problem,
I turn my attention toward its solution.

Taking action is a form of focus that leads to manifestation.

Turning my awareness toward an issue or person
increases its power so I am thoughtful
about where I focus my attention.

What I apply my attention to increases.

I find my own center
by focusing on the spirit within.

This is such an exciting principle and one which many people don't understand. The simple fact is that by focusing on what we don't like and what makes us angry or frustrated, we are sure to have more of that in our lives. The blessing is that when we focus on the positive in our world, we will create more of what is good for us. It is certainly appropriate to notice and discern what is not working in our world, but dwelling on it and worrying about it will not be helpful. Obviously, the mind's focus comes first, and in order to turn our focus into a tangible result, we need to take actions to achieve our desires. Therefore, we will receive great benefit by engaging this principle mindfully to tune into the positive.

26 COMPASSION

My heart is full of compassion for all

Compassionate love
pours from my heart.

I feel a great sympathy toward people
in need or in weakened positions.

I feel an empathy with all who suffer.

I want to reach out and hold in my arms
the poor, the sick and the suffering
and soothe their troubled souls.

My overwhelming sense of compassion
leads me to involvement and action.

I find ways to apply the yearnings of my heart
to help those for whom I am concerned.

My compassion extends to all in need,
whether I know them or not.

Compassion is the natural outpouring of a loving and open heart. When we understand that there is no separation between us, we will see others as a part of ourselves. What happens to the least of us happens to us as well. Cultivating compassion means letting go of only caring for our own family and friends and opening up to caring for all, no matter how we are related or not related. Turning a sense of compassion into involvement and support is an important component. Sharing and serving those in need should not come from a place of pity but will be more effective when offered with a sense of equality and empathy. When we turn our compassion into helpful action, all will benefit.

27 SUPPORT

I experience support in everything that happens

I see everything that happens to me as support.

I feel the constant support of the universe aligning my individual self with my higher self, the universal self.

I am learning to accept
even apparent negativity as support.

In the process, I benefit and
grow from all circumstances.

I give support to those in need and in turn,
I am supported when I am in need.

I reach deep inside where I experience
the true nature of support.

I may not always understand the form support comes in, but I choose to receive anything that happens to me as support and I feel blessed by it.

This principle of seeing everything as support runs contrary to what we are taught to believe. We usually think that something we like is supportive and what we don't like isn't. However, when we can truly see that everything that happens can lead to something positive, we will learn that all is support. If certain people rub us the wrong way, we need to also see them as being supportive because they are in fact letting us know where we are still sensitive and in what areas we need to strengthen ourselves. When we master this principle of seeing all as support, we will be creating a life for ourselves that works in the best possible way and allows more of the goodness of life to come our way.

28 NON-JUDGMENT

I am letting go of my critical nature

I am learning to overcome my critical nature.

I acknowledge the difference between
judgment and discernment.

I am turning off the constant
'I like it'/'I don't like it' inner conversation
and coming more from a place of acceptance of all that is.

As I let go of my judgments and prejudices,
I find that I attract more positive people
and experiences into my life.

I realize that when I focus on what I don't like,
I attract that into my life.

I instead choose to focus on what works for me
and let go of what doesn't work.

With practice, I find I am able to create the life I want.

We are so used to living in an on-off, yes-no, like it-don't like it, digital universe, that we think that is the only way to be. We will be pleasantly surprised with the results when we learn to minimize the judgmental aspects of our mind. This is not to say that we shouldn't be discerning about things that require introspection. We certainly do need to make appropriate choices, yet we will benefit when we learn to maintain a balanced temperament at all times. Cultivating non-judgment will have the added bonus of helping to create a life that flows more smoothly and attracts situations to us that we appreciate. We will especially benefit when we learn to stop judging ourselves and those closest to us.

29 NON-VIOLENCE

I am overcoming violence in my world

I strive to overcome violence in myself,
in my thoughts, my words and my actions.

I recognize the potency of my thoughts so I am
learning to overcome negative thinking.

I replace negative thoughts with positive, supportive ideas.

I work to react to crises and injustices
with solutions and positive responses.

I am learning to manage my communications
and relationships with skill and tact.

As I do so, I am building a community
of support that will overcome violence.

I realize as I transform my own inner landscape,
I am transforming the aggressive tendencies in my world.

We tend to think of violence as primarily a physical condition, but we need to be aware of its non-physical, mental aspects as well. We more easily recognize violence in its grosser forms, but it is the more subtle, internal violence of our thoughts that can be insidious and personally harmful. Therefore, we must be vigilant in perusing our mental landscape to root out any residue of violent patterning. We must be especially careful to not react violently to the violence and imbalances of others or we have defeated our goal of becoming a peaceful person. As we transform our own inner nature, we will naturally share the blessings of peace with the world around us and all will benefit.

30 MIRACLES

I am blessed with the miracle of life

Life is a miracle and I feel blessed
to be part of that miracle.

I open myself to miracles,
both large and small.

I experience miracles occurring
with increasing frequency in my life
as I keep my focus in the present moment.

I realize the interconnected web of life is
a constantly changing living system
that can provide solutions and
opportunities at the perfect moment.

I surrender to the timely manifestation of
extraordinary events, amazing situations and phenomenal
people to come forth and support my life process.

How often we forget what a gift life is in all its many and diverse facets. When we can stay focused on the miracle of everyday existence, we open ourselves to magic occurring more regularly in our lives. We can have fun with this principle when we recognize our partnership with the universe that puts people and situations before us that we hadn't even dreamed of or considered. The ever-changing sea of infinite possibilities moves and shapeshifts itself in ways that helps us along on our path. When we are afraid or stuck in negativity, the sea of possibilities freezes and we lose the opportunity for a miracle to present itself. Appreciation of the miracle of life will keep us open and our options fluid.

31 KINDNESS

I treat everyone with kindness

My way of being is kindness.

I treat everyone in my life with kindness,
whether they are family members, co-workers
or people I don't even know.

By exuding kindness in all directions, I am
bathed in gentle waves of support and love.

I am caring and gentle in my dealings with people,
whether or not they are considerate of me.

I act and speak in a way that shows
I care about others and go out of my way
to help those in need and enjoy their positive reaction.

Loving-kindness is the essence of who I am.

We like to think that kindness is a significant part of our character, but often we find ourselves acting in ways that are less than kind. When we notice we are grumpy, critical or unloving to family and friends, we need to remind ourselves to pump up the kindness factor. We need to be patient with ourselves when we observe ourselves acting unkindly and be vigilant in overcoming those tendencies. It is often a case of habit or imitative patterning that we may have inherited from our parents or others in our lives. With people who are close to us, we are often lazy and let these negative propensities take over. Instead, we should try to treat everyone as we would someone we most respect.

32 PATIENCE

I am becoming more patient every day

I cultivate patience in my life.

I notice that I am able to deal with challenges
or delays without becoming upset or annoyed.

I calmly persevere
when faced with events beyond my control.

I do not let pain or hurt provoke me
to complain or become frustrated.

I maintain serenity in the face of problems and in so doing,
I find that whatever was a challenge before, gradually
diminishes or goes away.

As I persist in maintaining a sense of calmness
in spite of external events, I find that the quality
of my inner being is greatly enhanced.

Patience is a true key to so many aspects of self-improvement. When we exercise patience for others, we are better able to get along. When we are patient with ourselves, we experience a greater degree of self-love. When we can learn to accept what life gives us with a sense of calmness and patience, we will be able to get through tough times and even painful circumstances. Cultivating a sense of calmness in the face of intense or traumatic situations may be a saving grace and help us to survive and ultimately thrive despite our difficulties. As we develop true patience, we will be blessed with improvements in our life and our relationships that will be deep and enduring.

33 RESPECT

I have a deep respect for all beings

I show respect and consideration for people around me
no matter their age, race, sex, or position.

Everyone I come across
receives my thoughtful consideration.

In turn, I act in such a way that
garners respect from others.

By being reliable and trustworthy and
by generously honoring others,
I notice that mutual respect is increasing around me.

In addition to my concern for people,
I also respect the earth and nature
for all it gives to support my life.

I respect the divine spirit of life
and seek a balance in all my dealings
with people and the planet.

Respect works in all directions. When we respect others, they will most likely respect us. When we respect ourselves, others will naturally respect us. Respect going out to all, without preconceived notions of position or posture, will return magnified to the one giving it. We can demonstrate our level of respect for people and the environment by practicing mindfulness. This powerful consciousness tool will keep us from mishaps and inadvertent mistakes. Thus, we think before we act and let our actions be born of thoughtful inquiry. A parent respecting a child is as important as a child respecting a parent. When people feel respected they will act accordingly, rising to the expectation.

34 EMPOWERMENT

I am one with the power of the Universe

I am empowered
to be the best person I can be.

By turning my focus deep within,
I access hidden reservoirs of strength that
help me to accomplish what I set out to do

I do not wait for others to give me the power,
but rather I accept the spiritual force
that I know exists inside me.

As I gain confidence in my innate power,
I am sensitive toward others and strive to
support them to feel empowered as well.

Through mutual support, we achieve a
sense of personal empowerment and confidence.

When we learn to tap into the innate power within the **core of our very being, we discover an infinite source of free energy.**

This power center is fueled by our breath which is activated by a human bellows, the diaphragm, pumping air in and out continuously for as long as we are alive.

It is stunning to realize the strength of this engine at our center of our existence.

It is constantly generating energy and transforming oxygen to fuel, to waste, and back again. And that is only the physical aspect of our power. The psycho-spiritual levels of our empowerment are much greater and more of a mystery. On a personal level, we each are able to access a reservoir of power to meet the needs of any situation.

35 BALANCE

I easily balance all aspects of my life

My life is in a natural state of balance.

I create a healthy balance between
work and play, relaxation and activity,
social time and alone time.

I notice if I am overworked
or overwhelmed in my life,
and I strive to regain my sense of balance
by taking time off or making space for inner work.

I look at all aspects of my life and acknowledge
where I need to find the balance.

I look at the physical, emotional,
mental and spiritual aspects of my being
and work toward bringing them all
into a peaceful state of equilibrium.

Life is an interplay of choices, pluses and minuses, decisions to be made. We go through our days and years deciding what to do with our time and resources. When we realize that we are truly masters of our lives, we can make choices that will benefit us. As we bring all aspects of our life into balance, we may sometimes feel pulled in different directions due to outside circumstances and pressures. To balance disparate opinions, we need to evaluate information coming in based on the core values of our heart. We put our dreams into action by honestly weighing our options and making informed decisions that bring about equilibrium. When we access inner balance, we are able to act from that place and succeed at life.

36 HARMONY

I am in harmony with my world

I am bringing all aspects of my being into harmony.

When I have internal harmony, I am better able to create peace and harmony in the world around me.

When I notice conflict in my relationships, I look at how I can contribute to bringing them back into alignment.

When I see dissonant relationships or conflict, I gently offer my harmonizing support.

By looking for sources of agreement and accord, I am better able to find the harmony that exists beyond the differences.

Through appreciation of diversity, we create a more beautiful symphony in the concert of our lives.

In order for harmony to exist, there needs to be a certain amount of agreement among the players. That does not mean that everyone plays the same note, but it does require a pleasing combination and interplay of notes. Thus, we find ways to create relationships that work well together and have intervals that aren't dissonant. When we notice dissonant relationships or conflicts, we work to help bring them into harmony and agreement. Ultimately, we want to live in peace so seeking harmony in our lives is a way to reach that state We each offer a unique tone and expression and by listening to one another and making minor adjustments, we find ways of fitting together in harmony.

37 COMMUNICATION

I speak my truth clearly and kindly

I strive for valid communication
by tuning into others.

In listening, I take the first step toward
understanding and being understood.

I speak my truth with compassion, always
trying to respect the other person's position.

My goal is for clarity and compassionate perspective,
even if differences exist.

I am persistent in the process of keeping
channels of communication open and clear.

When difficulties arise,
I am patient with myself and others,
knowing that if I stay present, the appropriate
words will be found to create understanding.

In our desire to be heard and understood, we need to listen with an open mind to the expression of others. When we are clear and transparent in our expression, we lay the foundation for understanding. The words we say are backed up by the feelings they carry. Simply getting our own ideas out is not the point of valid communication. Rather, it is important to strive for clarity for all parties to be understood. When someone is not able to clearly express themselves or does not feel listened to, often frustration and anger result. To avoid those negative reactions, we can work toward making sure everyone has their say and receives a thoughtful hearing. With respectful listening, there will be understanding.

38 GIVING & RECEIVING

The more I give the more I receive

Life is arranged in a perfect
relationship of giving and receiving.

I breathe in oxygen that the plants exhale,
and they breathe in the carbon dioxide that I exhale.

It is a perfect symbiotic relationship.

I breathe in the life force,
I breathe out the life force.

I give love;
I receive love.

Giving and receiving love
has the greatest reward.

I give for the sake of giving
without expectation of return or reward.

The more I give, the more I receive
of life's abundant blessings.

Understanding the relationship between giving and receiving unlocks the doorway to creating fulfillment in our lives. When we have a sense of lack, we are defining ourselves in that context. By giving even when we may have little, we put ourselves in a position to receive. There is a balance in the process so when we are in need of love or of anything, we are best served by sending out love or giving what we can to others. It is important to give without expectation of recognition or return, for then it is truly a gift from the heart. We do not give in order to receive but because giving is our nature. We want to develop within us a giving spirit and from that place, all sorts of blessings will come our way.

39 ABUNDANCE

As I share the abundance, it increases

As each plant produces hundreds or thousands of seeds
that could become the fruit and then the tree,
so nature offers all we need to be alive and thrive.

We appreciate the prosperous Earth
which gives a bountiful harvest every season.

May we manage the abundance well
and caretake this eternal paradise
so it will continue to produce its bounty.

As the earth offers its abundance and I receive it,
I have everything I need and more.

I love sharing what I have which
enhances the flow of life's blessings.

There is great abundance in the world and by keeping it flowing, we help to enhance it and make it available to all. Recognizing how the process works by noticing it in the natural world will help us understand this principle. Nature produces more than enough to replenish itself and provide food and oxygen for all. There is enough for everyone, but if we hoard more than our fair share, we block the flow and ultimately limit it for ourselves as well. Thus, it works best when we focus on sharing the abundance with others, especially those in need. This is not about charity but about plugging into the natural order of reality where there is enough for everyone's needs, but not necessarily for everyone's greeds.

40 GOING WITH THE FLOW

I let go of expectations and go with the flow

Instead of resisting situations
I perceive as negative,
I flow through them
and out the other side.

In the process,
I become more clear about
the quality of life I really want,
and I begin to attract those kinds of events to me.

By going with the flow,
I experience life as it is given to me
and learn the lessons being offered,
even though I may not have realized I needed them.

In so doing,
I am better able to create my own reality.

It is exciting to truly understand this principle. By letting go of our resistance to negative events or people, we can actually release them from having power over us. We can't always control the details of what happens to us but we can control our reaction to them. To the contrary, when we tighten our resistance, we increase the negative effect of the situation and will have much more trouble dealing with it. By going with the flow, we can learn from the experience without being harmed by it. At the same time, we can be developing a more clear picture of the kind of life we truly want for ourselves and put our creative energy into manifesting and attracting situations to us that are in keeping with our vision.

41 SELF WORTH

I am a divine being of great value

I know my life has intrinsic value.

I am a divine being
and my life is a gift that I treasure.

I believe in myself and don't let
others affect my opinion of myself.

I do accept feedback when appropriate
without taking it personally.

I welcome any information that can
help me become a better person.

If I notice qualities about myself that I don't care for,
I work toward changing them without judging myself
for having those qualities.

My confidence and self-esteem are growing
as I honor and respect the person I am.

What we feel about ourselves is of paramount importance to our health and well being on both physical and spiritual levels. What we say to ourselves internally is what we become. Therefore, the quality of our self-talk is extremely important and ultimately determines who we are. We need to carefully sort out the messages we have been given about ourselves from others and the messages we have been choosing to tell ourselves. Then we can become clear on what we really want to be telling our inner being. When we can accept the divine aspect of who we are and honor the needs of our physical being as well, we will be that much closer to becoming the best person we can be, a truly divine being.

42 HOPE

I have realistic hope for my world

I have high hopes for myself and my world.

By being hopeful, I am not avoiding reality, but rather,
I am giving a positive direction to my life.

I am always looking to see the good
in other people and in events that occur.

By focusing on the positive, even in apparently
negative situations, I am able to transform
what is happening in a constructive way.

My optimistic approach to life is contagious,
and I find that people around me are gradually
becoming more encouraged about their future.

Together, we are creating the
kind of world we want to live in.

Being hopeful will lead us in the direction we want to go. Being fearful will lead us in the direction of our fears. Which way do we want to go? By staying positive and always expecting the best, we set ourselves up for a much better chance at a positive future. An optimistic spirit will carry us a lot further than a pessimistic one and will make us more welcome in people's lives. At the same time, we want to be grounded in reality so taking positive actions to improve conditions in our world will bring our hopes and realities closer together. As we creatively transform ourselves from within, we will find that we have a positive effect on the people around us and ultimately will transform our world.

43 JUSTICE

I trust that justice exists in the world

I trust that justice is inevitable
in the overall scheme of things.

As I strive to be fair and reasonable
in my dealings with others,
I realize I am contributing to the presence
of justice in the world.

I also know that justice is a condition
that often needs strong advocates
and I am willing to work hard to
bring forth justice where it is needed.

I remain positive even in the face
of obvious injustices and use my highest principles
to counteract the forces
of greed and selfishness in the world.

Sometimes the facts of life seem to indicate otherwise, but the truth remains that justice is certain to prevail in the long run. When viewed only in the short term, it is often easy to miss, but with patience and perseverance, we will inevitably find a fair outcome.

That does not mean when we notice unfairness or inhumane treatment by others that we should ignore it.

It is not only the passage of time that will bring about change, but it is through our human commitment and accessing our highest principles that we can bring about justice.

By acting in fair and just ways ourselves, we are contributing to making justice a reality in our world. As we rally our forces and take action, we help to manifest justice.

44 INTEGRITY

I am honest and truthful in all my dealings

I operate from a place of inner
integrity and moral principles.

I am honest and truthful
in my dealings with others.

I honor the innate reality and wholeness
of my own life as I perceive it.

I speak my truth with
compassion and sincerity.

I do what I say I will do and people
respect me and trust my word.

When I communicate, it is from a place of
clarity and integrity and I attract relationships
that are honest and down to earth.

When we can be completely honest with ourselves, we are best able to create a life of integrity around us. This can take some deep soul searching to discover the truth within us, but once recognized, it becomes the foundation for our honor and morality. Then when we speak, we are coming from a place of inner integrity. The more we live up to our word and follow through on our commitments, the more others will respect us and reflect those same principles back to us. As we develop clarity on the truth within us, we will discover that we attract people and events to us that support the fulfillment of that truth. By choosing to live by the highest moral standards, we see the best possible life unfold for us.

45 NATURAL ORDER

I honor the natural order of all life

Nature has an inherent natural order.

Sometimes I understand it
and sometimes I don't.

Yet, still, I rest assured in the
perfection and order of natural systems.

I am part of that divine order as are all beings.

I open myself to thinking and
acting in ways that are in harmony
with the natural order of the universe.

When I look at just a part of
what is happening in my life,
I may not see the perfection.

Instead, I try to see each event and
situation as part of a greater whole and
trust that it fits perfectly in the scheme of my life.

We exist within the natural order of the universe whether we notice it or not. Our bodies are designed to work perfectly and only when we distance ourselves from our true nature do we open the way for sickness and disease to enter. The more we can attune ourselves with this natural order, the greater will our chances be to take full advantage of the gifts that life has bestowed upon us. As we reflect on the beauty and harmony of natural systems, we can learn how we can best fit into those systems. Whether at macroscopic or microscopic levels, there is a divine blueprint that can be understood and followed. When we are able to examine these systems, we will see the perfection that exists everywhere.

46 RESPONSIBILITY

I take full responsibility for everything that happens to me

I take responsibility for my actions and
strive to act in responsible ways at all times.

I am accountable for what occurs
as a result of my actions and I even
accept responsibility for what happens to me
as a result of other people's actions.

I don't blame others when
things don't seem to go my way.

By taking responsibility for
everything that happens to me,
I find I am able to have much greater
control over the direction of my life.

By being responsive to my world,
I am able to shape it in ways that work for me.

By taking responsibility for everything that happens to us, we are empowered to make improvements at will. If there is something in our world not to our liking, we can assume full responsibility for transforming it into something more suitable. When we even take responsibility for what happens to us that may have been caused by others, we are not allowing ourselves to be victims but rather we are empowering ourselves as masters of our universe and fully in charge of our personal destiny. We recognize that people need to be held accountable for their actions and we begin by holding ourselves accountable. From personal responsibility grows a responsible family, community, nation and world.

47 INNER BEAUTY

I cultivate the beauty of my inner being

I look at the inner beauty of myself and others,
rather than seeing only surface levels of being.

I appreciate the qualities that reflect
love, compassion and support.

I don't judge myself or others
for physical attributes, but instead look
deep within to see the soul
and spirit of the person.

As I connect with others on a soul level,
I am developing the spiritual aspect of myself as well.

By focusing at deep levels of being,
my own inner beauty is enhanced.

Our world is so focused on the material and physical that we often don't look deeply to see the true beauty of the inner soul. We may carry judgments about our own bodies or the physical qualities of others and miss the opportunity to appreciate the deeper nature of the spirit. Instead, we will be better served to notice how a person speaks and acts in order to see the reflection of who they truly are. When we act kindly and compassionately, we are displaying a spiritual beauty which includes those qualities that are attractive to others. These aspects are the ones that will help us attract a friend or lover and support us in creating enduring relationships based on our values and principles.

48 CHANGE

I accept the transformative nature of change

I honor the inevitability of change.

Life is a process of constant transformation and
I am learning to flow with what happens in my world.

When I let go of my resistance to change,
I find that often something better comes along.

I ride change like a roller coaster,
even with its ups and downs,
knowing it all works out if I don't resist.

The improvements that come with change are a welcome gift.

Just because I accept change doesn't mean
I am destined to never have stability.

On the contrary, my life is grounded and enduring.

Since change comes whether we want it or not, we might as well get used to it. If we can't keep change away, we can at least find ways to flow with it. One good technique to make the most out of transformational times is to genuinely welcome the opportunity that change is presenting. When we surprise change by not resisting it and actually welcoming it, we get to participate in its dance and end up benefiting after all. Change can be a breath of fresh air inhaled into a situation, blowing things around and shaking up the world. During the process, we become transformed by our reaction to what is happening. How we react to changing times and transformational tides determines our character.

49 GUIDANCE

I am open to guidance in whatever form it comes

I am open to receiving guidance
in whatever form it comes.

I especially open to my higher self or angelic self
so that I may receive divine guidance for
the many decisions I make along the path of my life.

By adhering to my highest principles,
I find that I am in a position to be divinely directed
to make the perfect choices that achieve
the highest benefit for all.

I ask for guidance that will
benefit others as well as myself.

When I clear and quiet my mind,
I find I am best able to receive
the ideal direction for my life.

The first step toward receiving guidance into one's life is to invite it in. Too often we assume we know what is best for us and don't consider asking for guidance from a higher power. Whether we call it god, angels, higher self, subconscious mind or the universe, we can benefit by seeking guidance. When we open ourselves to guidance, we are making a space for the right information to come to us that can help us along our path. We don't have to make the decisions of our lives alone when we know how to ask for and receive guidance. Working in partnership will help us stay on track for the ideal direction of our lives.

50 BLISS

I let my spirit soar with eternal bliss

I access a place deep inside me
of spiritual joy.

I recognize that this state of untroubled happiness
is not dependent on external events but rather
is my inherent state of eternal bliss.

As I learn to live by
my highest principles and values,
I have greater awareness
of this heavenly state within me.

I nurture this feeling of well being,
especially in situations that appear to be negative.

I rejoice and celebrate my ability to rise
above any difficult circumstances and in so doing,
I find that life unfolds in a much more positive direction.

True bliss is not dependent on anything in the external world but is an expression of an inner joy that has roots in eternity. When we allow ourselves the freedom to experience spiritual joy, we find that our happiness comes from a source deep within us and cannot be touched or diminished by external factors. It is good to practice reaching this state during untroubled times so one can more readily achieve it during times of trials and tribulations. Staying grounded is essential as the expression of bliss can range from ecstatic joy to deep inner peace and along a continuum in between. When fully developed, one may achieve a continuous state of bliss that is independent from outside circumstances.

51 SACRED STILLNESS

I access the sacred stillness at the core of my being

As I clear and quiet my mind,
I surrender to the sacred stillness within me.

I let myself be bathed in its soft sweetness.

I breathe in deeply and find
at the center of my being,
the very essence of who I am.

I recognize the sacredness that is my eternal self.

In this peaceful moment of understanding,
I feel my connection with the
consciousness at the core of all life.

I feel the oneness with all that is.

As I go through my days and nights,
expressing my individuality and gifts,
I often return to this place of sacred stillness
to refresh and revitalize myself.

A Year of Guided Meditations

As we learn to calm our bodies and quiet our minds, we allow the soul to find its way home to the truth of who we are. When we can let go of the distractions and temptations of the physical world, we are able to experience the true union of our soul with the universal oneness from which we come. This precious place of inner quiet is a pool of infinite wisdom. When we can experience the sacred silence, we are able to get in touch with the essence of who we are. In this sacred place, we connect with not just our own being, but we also have access to the greater consciousness that pervades the universe. Through practice, we can return to this quiet place whenever we want.

52 SLEEP

I welcome the soothing rejuvenation of sound sleep

I let go of the busyness of my day and fall
gently asleep at the appropriate time.

I realize that good sleep is necessary
for the full functioning of my body and soul.

I am learning to clear my mind and
relax my body so sleep comes to me naturally.

I allow myself to be gently soothed
into a deep, relaxing sleep.

I welcome the positive dreams to take me
away to a gentle place in my imagination.

Sleep is my friend and comes easily to me when I am ready,
carrying me off to a place of soothing relaxation.

I rest in sleep as long as needed.

When complete, I awaken refreshed
and revitalized, ready for a new day.

Whether we are falling asleep for the night or taking a much-needed rest during the day, we can learn to relax our bodies and let go of the busy activity of our mental processes. In this state of rest, we are free from mental or emotional anxiety and the body is able to restore itself. Even if falling asleep has been difficult in the past, with practice and the support of soft music and gentle words, we can train ourselves to release the ties that bind us to our waking world. As we learn to fall gently asleep at will, we will find that the refreshing nature of a good sleep will allow us to function at a much higher capacity when we are awake. We then achieve a healthy balance between waking and sleeping.

DUDLEY EVENSON is a best-selling author, multi-media producer, harpist, life coach, and photographer. She and her husband, Dean Evenson, are sound healing pioneers and have produced over 90 albums and videos since founding their label Soundings of the Planet in 1979. Over the years, they have shared their music and guided meditations before such noted authors as Deepak Chopra, Joan Borysenko, Larry Dossey, Iyanla Vanzant, Denise Linn and don Miguel Ruiz.

For decades, Dudley and Dean have been on the cutting edge of music and media that heals and uplifts, consistently taking people to a place where peace prevails. Their motto, *Peace Through Music,* is reflected in their inspiring music of flute, harp and natural sounds which has been used in hospitals, prisons, schools, yoga, massage and spiritual centers to support people's healing or life process. Since 1970, they've also produced numerous videos and documentaries, many of which can be seen on their two YouTube channels: *Soundings of the Planet* and *Soundings Mindful Media.*

Related Releases by **Dean Evenson & Dudley Evenson**

QUIETING THE MONKEY MIND: HOW TO MEDITATE WITH MUSIC
(160 pages with full-color photos and illustrations)
Available as: Paperback • E-book

A YEAR OF GUIDED MEDITATIONS: 52 WEEKLY AFFIRMATIONS *Available as:* DVD

MEDITATION MOMENT: 52 WEEKLY AFFIRMATIONS
Available as: Spoken Word CD • Download • Streaming

MEDITATION MOODS *Available as:*
Flute/Harp CD • Download • Streaming

Music, Blog, Podcast & Social Links visit:
www.soundings.com